Soul Be Free III

Different Hues of The Blues

Soul Be Free III

Different Hues of The Blues

ALFONSO & OUIDA C. WYATT

Soul Be Free III
Different Hues of The Blues

© 2018
Alfonso & Ouida C. Wyatt

Published by

The Power of Hope Press

ISBN: 978-1-932842-88-3

*The Power of Hope Press seeks to publish books
drawn from actual life experiences
that educate, edify, and inspire.*

Printed in the United States of America

PREFACE

I remember sitting at the breakfast table when Ouida broached the idea that our next book in the Soul Be Free series should focus on mental illness. My mind pondered how could we address mental health issues and stay true to our past formula using creative expression as the driver to reveal transformational truths about self, life, and Spirit. The more we talked about the project, the more I saw that it was not only possible— it was needed. One of our major goals is to address the shame and stigma associated with mental illness. We went to work identifying our unpublished poems that addressed midnight of the mind issues. Then we took a different step by asking people to contribute their direct or indirect experiences dealing with mental health.

Some writers chose to use spoken word, or poetry; several used deep and personal testimonies, and one young person offered her artwork to complement her words. It was uplifting to hear similar cathartic responses each time we received their writings. We left submissions open to their interpretation, style, and personality so their voices and presenting styles were authentic. Their soul-bearing words were insightful, humbling and awe-inspiring. The creativity we sought evidenced itself when it was time to position poems and writings in a manner intended to enlighten, engage and encourage readers. What I could not see at the breakfast table is what I am writing about right now: *Soul Be Free III: Different Hues of The Blues*—the vision is truly for an appointed time.

FOREWORD

Sonia R. Banks, Ph.D., LCP

Discovering the impact of our mind's capacity to make meaning under the onslaught of life's daily challenges and struggles is what makes being human so complex. The development and protection of our mental health has always been at the heart of how we function and come to know our real selves. As we consider all that we ask of ourselves, and others, if we live long enough, we realize what it takes to survive our pain, sustain our capacity to live in spite of our trauma and to, somehow, turn our broken hearts into beautiful songs, stories and poems expressing our complex and carefully woven lives.

Soul Be Free III: Different Hues of The Blues, co-written by Rev. Dr. Alfonso Wyatt and Ouida C. Wyatt, so beautifully illustrates the gifts in the sadness that comes with life's pathways being chipped away. The authors offer us a way to see what lies beneath the façade of perceived social and psychological support through to the hardness that replaces hope during those dark days. I am so glad that they decided to write a book that uncovers the truth of what is really going on in the mental health of our sisters and brothers. Alfonso and Ouida lay bare the hearts and souls of those who must choose life and living over all the obstacles and odds against that choice.

In my practice and work as a licensed clinical psychologist in New York and Virginia, treating and consulting in and throughout various communities, corporations and organizations, I have discovered that all of us are asked to appear in our lives as stable, supported, healthy people. And we are not. The presented stories boldly offer the context of people surviving the darkness of their own minds and spirits and, yet, as I have seen in my practice, they reconcile themselves to continue the unrelenting and unquenchable desire to live-even with the tiniest light and the most devastating agony from memories and distorted beliefs people are holding. And some are not.

We have a lot of work ahead of us before real healing for mental health issues is taken seriously and afforded the space in the health discourse it deserves. I believe the way to start the work of creating a new mental health reality, is with truth telling and sharing. It is my belief this book will offer the type of reflective integration that pausing to meditate and contemplate always does. It helps to ask if the life that has chosen you is being recognized for all the gifts and opportunities it brings. From that awareness, I choose to believe readers will declare their own commitment to seek help—wherever it can be found and not stop seeking it until he or she is heard, helped, and invited into a loving healing community of sojourners maintaining good mental health.

Sonia R Banks, Ph.D., LCP, is an experienced clinical psychologist with extensive demonstrated expertise in psychotherapy and behavioral health interventions designed to reduce harmful behaviors. She has successfully incorporated a culturally congruent person-centered care approach to behavioral medicine for over eighteen years. Dr. Banks uses a resiliency model to diagnose, establish care plans and support networks that reinforce adjustments and innovative adaptations to treatment, coordinating prevention partners in academic institutions, public, not for profit, and faith-based organizations.

TABLE OF CONTENTS

Poems in lowercase by A. Wyatt
Poems in UPPERCASE by O.C.W.

The God of peace be with you all. Amen.
Romans 15:33 NIV

dark dialogue

fear

has become me
locked deep inside
choking my spirit
slowly killing
my will
to feel   to be
to hope   to live

strange

no longer
see life in colors
sun
sky
rainbow
all
in mourning
draped in
sad grey

voices

won't leave me alone
mind dulled
by the journey to nowhere
fixed on what
is not
what will never be
thoughts from
this
abyss
fighting
for equal time
sounds like me
talking to me

1

like I don't know me
like I don't love me
like I am lost inside me
saying
good-bye to me

accusing

day night twilight
not here
never there
who stole
my tears
one more thing
to think about

self

looks at self
then calls across
the room
will you   answer
will you   explain
will you   tell
how fear has
                become me

CRY FROM THE ABYSS
Rev. Dr. Alfonso Wyatt

—taken from *Strategic Destiny Dispatch* Vol. I. V.

I was once depressed during my mid-twenties. I still remember the feeling of being confused, alone and disconnected. I was dragged down to a dark place, encouraged by a stunning array of poor life decisions that finally caught up with me. I knew something was wrong but felt powerless to address available options that my mind, at the time, could not process. I felt trapped in a monochromatic grey world devoid of rhythm, definition, or sense of time. There was no exit. There was no relief—just more of the same diffused malaise. I was in the grip of a relentless invisible foe that would not show compassion, not even when it was painfully clear I was utterly and completely defeated—or so I thought.

So why is it so difficult to talk about depression? I think one reason is that people who have not been depressed may not fully understand what it is like not being able to feel, act, or react. The easiest thing to say to a depressed person is, "Snap out of it, shake it off, get back in the race, what's the matter with you," assuming there is an acquired weakness or lack of will contributing to their plight. I have a childhood friend who served this country in Vietnam. He told me almost as an aside, "Living with constant pain is depressing." In the same week, I counseled a young sister who broke up with her boyfriend after a betrayal with her best friend. At the time, the young woman was pregnant, alone, and depressed.

A psychiatrist friend recently conducted a study on depression in black men within the faith community. One of his findings is that more men are clinically depressed (and will not go for help) than women. Could it be that males (of all ages) are expected to handle their pain (anger) stoically as an indicator of their manhood? Some depressed people tend to suffer in silence, or in plain sight, surrounded by well-meaning, caring people who may have formed a sympathetic attachment to the depressed individual but who will not take direct action to intervene for whatever reason.

There is a dire psychological, social and spiritual cost associated with keeping emotions tightly bottled up inside. This is a good time to thank a dear sister, friend, and colleague, Terrie Williams, for writing, *Black Pain: It Just Looks Like We're Not Hurting*. Her personal testimony and book on depression has helped many people suffering in shame and silence. Here is a thought-provoking excerpt from *Black Pain*.

> A depressed Black man doesn't necessarily look like he's "down in the dumps," "cryin' the blues," or any of the other clichés we use to describe what depression looks like. A depressed Black man might be the most energetic man you know, a ball of fire who never stops moving or doing, whether or not the moving gets him anywhere or the doing does anything. A depressed Black man might be accomplished in all kinds of socially acceptable areas (career, church, sports, and school), or he might be the kind of man who cannot stop making everything worse for himself and anyone who loves him...

If you are depressed, find the strength to get help. You do not have to suffer in silence. You may know relatives, spouses, churchgoers, sorority/fraternity members, colleagues, car-poolers, youth—all crying out from the abyss of depression. Can you hear—or, are you the one in pain? Either way...get help.

WHEN SUNNY GETS BLUE

WHEN
SUNNY
GETS
BLUE
WHO PLACED THAT CLOAK ON YOU
STITCHED WITH SHAME
NOT YOUR REAL NAME
JUST HOW YOU GONNA GET UP
WHEN THE WORD IS OUT
ABOUT WHAT YOU WILL NEVER BE
CAN'T SEE
WHAT PUT THAT SLUMP IN
YOUR SHOULDERS
OR
THAT ACHE IN YOUR BACK
THERE ARE SHADOWS
AROUND YOU
TIGHTENING
PRESSING YOU
WHEN WILL THE SHADOWS LEAVE
CAUGHT IN A HAZE OF MALAISE
A WEB OF GLOOM
WHEN
SUNNY
GETS
BLUE

LEARNING TO FLY
Sabrina Evans Ellis

I will never forget the day that, after 47 years, two degrees, an accomplished career as executive director of a non-profit, numerous successes and accolades; I realized that I was not stupid.

I took my oldest daughter, then nine, to have a neuropsychological evaluation for a suspected learning disability. As part of the initial consultation, the doctor asked us a series of questions to determine what battery of tests she should pursue. As the doctor asked questions about attention and hyperactivity, a strange pattern emerged. My daughter would respond that the symptom was not something she was experiencing, but one that she did observe in her sister. Stranger still, I noticed that not only were these symptoms present in my youngest daughter, but in myself.

"Do you have trouble paying attention, even when someone is speaking directly to you?"

"No, not really, but definitely my sister."
(And me...)

"Do you have trouble keeping track of tasks and activities?"

"No, not really, but definitely my sister."
(And me...)

"Do you have outbursts of anger at inappropriate times?"
"No, not really, but definitely my sister."
(And me...)

After the interview, my daughter went to sit in the waiting room while I conferred with the doctor. She said, "It seems like your oldest daughter does have a learning disability, and it also sounds like I need to see your youngest daughter as well-from what you have both said, she is showing signs of ADHD [Attention Deficit Hyperactivity Disorder]."

I hesitated and then quietly asked the doctor, "What does it mean that most of the questions you asked about ADHD were true for me as well?" She smiled and said, "I wouldn't be surprised, ADHD is often inherited— I expect that it would come from you or your husband. I can test you as well."

I left the office with a sense of inner turmoil…and peace; uncertainty, and an epiphany; fear and excitement. When I got home I called my mother—"Mom, you won't believe this—the doctor thinks Claire may have ADHD and she thinks she got it from me—I may have ADHD!"

My mother's response was definitive, "No you don't. You were not a fidgety child who couldn't sit down."

"But mom, symptoms are different in girls than in boys. Listen to the symptoms I found online:

• Starting projects, but moving on to the next thing that catches your interest before finishing.

• Messy or disorganized in multiple settings such as work and home

• Avoiding or delaying getting started on a task that requires a lot of thought.

• Trouble paying attention to boring or repetitive tasks.

• Misplacing things at home or at work."

My mom answered quickly, "Oh yes, you've been that way your whole life—is that ADHD?"

My whole life…

My whole life I was frustrated that I wasn't neater or (fill in the blank to describe the ever-changing inadequacy). I experienced: the annoyance of my parents, teachers, family members, friends, and co-workers who "tsk-tsked" at my frequently messy room/dorm/ apartment/ office and reliable tardiness; the never-ending shame, guilt and anxiety of never quite feeling on top of things, or up to par; the anger and jealousy I felt towards others who could do what I seemingly couldn't—my sister who was neat, other college co-eds who started their term projects weeks in advance as I delayed and avoided and then inexplicably scrambled at the last minute; co-workers who always responded to emails immediately and completed tasks easily and efficiently; bewilderment at my inability to focus on the most pressing of tasks—even under deadline; punishing myself by staying at work until 10 PM because I felt guilty about not being more focused during normal work hours.

But most of all I experienced judgment, "What is wrong with you? Why can't you (fill in the blank to describe the ever-changing inadequacy)?" I endured the pain and the embarrassment of consistently disappointing or frustrating others. "Why are you always late—you don't respect my time." "If you don't improve the timeliness of your performance your company will lose the contract." "You are a mother now, what kind of example are you setting by keeping your house this messy?" Or, as one of my daughter's teacher admonished me after excessive lateness, "Being late says something about who you are as a person..." The shame, guilt and anxiety often spiraled into severe depression, paralyzing anxiety, and infinite apologies, "I'm sorry, forgive the delay. I didn't mean to. I'm sorry—I'm trying..."

I followed through on the testing and the evaluation confirmed my suspicions—ADHD (inattentive type), depression, and anxiety. The doctor's recommendation—address the ADHD and the accompanying low-executive function skills and you may decrease the depression and anxiety. I sat down with my newly diagnosed youngest daughter, then seven, who was worried about this 'ADHD thing.'

"What does it mean mommy?" We discussed the symptoms and, I shared with her that I too had it. I watched the familiar weight lifting from her shoulders. "Is this why I have trouble with my temper and why I lose things? And why I feel bored all the time?"

"Yes."

She smiled. "I have ADHD Mommy! We have ADHD! I'm not stupid!"

"No, sweetie, we are not stupid or lazy, or incompetent, or a bad person. We have challenges and we can work on navigating those challenges so we can live better-and we can do this together."

Sometime later, I came across this Albert Einstein quote:

Everybody is a genius. But if you judge a fish by its ability to climb a tree, it will live its whole life believing that it is stupid.

As I read the quote, I thought about how long I had perceived myself as stupid. I ignored my own talents and gifts—my unique "genius" because in a society that rightfully values timeliness, organization, accountability, and focus, I had decided that, by that measure, I was indeed stupid, incompetent, inadequate, and ultimately unworthy of everything that I had accomplished. But, on that day, and every day since, I have begun to forgive myself for my shortcomings; work on accepting, addressing, and moving beyond my real challenges; appreciate my strengths and my capacity for change and growth; and to support my daughters in discovering their own genius. In short, I realized that this fish may not have legs to climb a tree, but I can grow wings and learn to fly.

Sabrina Evans-Ellis is a youth development and organizational development specialist who has provided technical assistance to nonprofit agencies for over 20 years. Her experience in the field includes direct service, program administration, leadership and management training, strategic planning and fund development. Sabrina is currently Executive Director of the Youth Development Institute. Sabrina's previous positions include: Senior Consultant at the Community Resource Exchange; Director of Out-of-School-Time Professional Development at Ramapo for Children; Deputy Director of Youth and Education Services for the St. Nick's Alliance; and faculty member at The Institute for Non-Profit Management at the Columbia University School of Business. Sabrina holds a Master's Degree in Communication Studies from the University of North Carolina at Chapel Hill.

LET THE HEALING BEGIN

A TURNAROUND FROM WITHIN
WITHOUT JUDGMENT
A WAY TO BEGIN
TIME TRAVEL KNOWING
HOW GOING THROUGH
RESCUED ME
AT FIRST
THE FEELING
COULDN'T KEEP
PACE WITH MYSELF
LET IT OUT
LET IT IN
VOICES ATTACK
GRACE DEFENDS
NOW LET THE
HEALING BEGIN
THERE IS AN END
TO THE CURRENT
STRONG CURRENT
AN EXPIRATION
AND DUE DATE
SIMULTANEOUSLY
DEATH BIRTHING
BEYOND THE CURRENT
CRACKED SHELL
THERE IS A RAY
OF LIGHT
IN
THE DARKNESS
BREAK THROUGH
LET THE
HEALING
BEGIN

~~Dear~~ Depression,

Get thee behind me and stay there!

You made me not think clearly; not be able to make decisions. You made me feel sad all the time, hopeless, like I was in a fog with the world continuing to go on without me. You gave me anxiety. It seemed like you came out of nowhere. Were you a delayed reaction to my mom's death two years prior? Were you the manifestation of insecurity and low self-esteem that finally came to a head? You got progressively worse to the point where you made me feel like I was in a deep, dark hole from which I couldn't escape. You made me sleep all day and not have an appetite. You made me not want to live. That was your first attack.

Hands being "laid on me" didn't lift you away. Prayers didn't make me better overnight. You caused me not to be able to read my Bible or listen to a sermon or worship. You made me believe that cries and pleas to the Lord for deliverance weren't heard. You had me thinking that God's presence wasn't with me. You made me think that death would be better than life. They told me you are a chemical imbalance in my brain that can be triggered. They said that after two bouts of clinical depression, I'd need to take medication to keep you at bay.

Since that first episode — you attacked me a few more times — even after you hadn't attacked me in over 10 years. This time you even added insomnia to the mix. Why did you come back? Hadn't I beaten you? Depression, maybe you are my "thorn in the flesh" like Paul, who asked God to take his thorn away. But you know what, Depression? — God said, "My grace is sufficient and that His strength is made complete in my weakness."

Depression, you attacked me, but you also attacked some mighty men mentioned in the Bible that God used: Elijah — the bold prophet of God, David — a man after God's own heart; Job, who lost everything but to whom God greatly restored in the end, and Jeremiah, a prophet who God used to speak His message to Israel. Depression, did you know that what you meant for evil, God would turn around to use for good? But, when you had me in your grip — I couldn't see that. Nevertheless, Depression, didn't you know that I overcome by the blood of the Lamb, the Word of my testimony?

Depression, you have a stigma. A stigma that makes me wonder when I'm completing my medical history form at my new doctor's office whether or not to disclose that I am taking antidepressants for fear that I'll be judged or thought of being crazy. Hopefully, though, that stigma will dissipate as more and more people are coming out and talking about their experience with you — celebrities, doctors, preachers, service men and women, and even psychiatrists. Maybe one day you'll be seen as a "real" disease just like diabetes or cancer.

Depression, you thought you defeated me, but God didn't let you.

Depression, although you made me feel like I was alone — the Lord said He would never leave me or forsake me. And, in addition to the Lord, I have loving and supportive family and friends who prayed for me and with me, who supported me and got me the help I needed, even when they couldn't understand. Depression, when you made me think I'd never be able to return to work again, God showed you that was a lie, and this year I'll be at my job 22 years despite the bouts I've had with you. Last year, I married my wonderful husband, who married me despite my battles with you because he saw past you.

Depression, I don't know if you'll show up again, and I am certainly not expecting you to. Since I can't change my history with you, I choose to use my experience to reach back and help strengthen others who are battling to overcome you, even as I continue to overcome you.

AGL is proud to be almost 50 years old, a first-time newlywed, and mother of an adult son. She is thankful to her parents for raising her in a loving, Christian home. AGL is a member of the multi-ethnic New Life Fellowship Church in Queens, NY. She is an administrator at a law school. She loves gospel music, 70s and 80s R&B, group exercise classes, the theatre, traveling and taking salsa lessons with her husband. AGL is grateful that she is unconditionally loved by God and seeks to love Him back with all her heart, mind, soul, and strength. AGL is happy to say that she is still here and enjoying a fulfilling life.

dreamer

chase your dreams
fast as you can
almost touched
by the dreamer's hand
over there
your dreams
oh so near
possess it before
it can disappear
dreams of hope
promises made
all begin to slowly fade
will you come
visit again
comfort me
your dreamer friend
soothe
my distracted mind
with
other
lost
dreams
you
find

KHAFRE EVELYN

One of my favorite people asked me to write about this disorder. I said yes right away. Five days before it was due, I found I didn't like any of the four lines I wrote. I really couldn't find the words to express what it's like being this way on a daily basis. All the trials & tribulations on this journey have really left me speechless because it is still something I am learning to cope with. I look back on my life and can never really grasp where it all went wrong. Just a bunch of empty questions and what ifs that echoes in my mind.

I'd be lying if I said I was indifferent because I can still feel the fire burning in me when I reflect. It's rarely peaceful yet I'm eerily calm. I'm still in the process of redefining who I am, what matters most and why I'm still here. I feel like my mind has gone through a slaughterhouse in a horror movie these past few years. I want to let go, but I don't think I ever will. I have experienced mental warfare and it's made my outlook even darker. You know something is wrong when you know you fear heights more than you fear death and laugh about it.

I remember waking up in hospitals confused with no recollection of what happened. Nothing but empty rooms and silence with no one to talk to but yet so many questions to answer after swallowing the first pill. So many doctors I hated, so many therapists I talked to but didn't connect with at all. I was falling fast & began to pinball around the city's hospitals. I was still rejecting medicine & trying to titrate my way off. I felt misunderstood. I felt like there was nothing wrong. I was in denial.

Khafre Evelyn is a freelance writer who is currently a student at Hostos Community College. This is his first published work. Khafre lives in Harlem, NY and is working on creating his first blog.

EULANI TUCKER

My name is Eulani Tucker and I am a 13-year-old artist. At the age of 10, I was diagnosed with Asperger's syndrome.* My interests are reading, music and playing video games. My passion is drawing warrior cats, dogs and cartoon characters. My dream is to be a professional artist/animator. Because I love to draw and animate over socializing, people think that I am an introvert. I am not, just bashful and selective with whom I choose to socialize. I'm a kind, caring and fun person. My struggle with being an Aspie sometimes makes me feel sad and angry. I have been told that God does not make any mistakes. This helps me feel better because Aspergians are extraordinary people who are gifted and talented, and most of all unique. And all of those adjectives are me, Eulani.

*Asperger syndrome is one of several previously separate subtypes of autism that were folded into the single diagnosis autism spectrum disorder (ASD) with the publication of the DSM-5 diagnostic manual in 2013. Asperger syndrome was generally considered to be on the "high functioning" end of the spectrum. Affected children and adults have difficulty with social interactions and exhibit a restricted range of interests and/or repetitive behaviors. Motor development may be delayed, leading to clumsiness or uncoordinated motor movements. Compared with those affected by other forms of ASD, however, those with Asperger syndrome do not have significant delays or difficulties in language or cognitive development. Some even demonstrate precocious vocabulary — often in a highly specialized field of interest.

(Asperger Syndrome Description Taken From Autism Speaks Website)

well spring

all hail the keeper
master of shattered dreams
minister of broken promises
the final ceremony
for those made bold
by madness
questioning the sanity
in pressing on

hear the keeper's words
coldly rationale
true liberation
will come
through self-destruction
clear a way for believers

behold
the heretics
they struggle for life
for peace of mind
finding strength
in spiritual waters
to
believe

FAITH IN A NEW LIFE

Antoinette Ann Acosta

A Rabbi once told me, "People view their world through their psychological lens." My father battled with depression and bi-polar disorder as long as four decades. He has made serious poor life choices. It's saddening because he was a beautiful man deep down, but his genetic makeup hindered him. It made me question people's willpower versus their illness. He also had an abusive father, who would hit him on the head on the ground very hard, take part in drugs, and sleep with females for money.

On the plus side, my father was intelligent; he was able to build computers from scratch, knew computer programming, construction, was an auto mechanic, handled electronics and he was spiritually gifted. He never finished college. He had so many aspirations. It saddens me that the same person could literally be "polar opposites" (making good and bad choices in a very steep way). I never knew when he would become stable. When he moved to a new location it helped, but he had to leave his past behind, which included me.

I love my father very much and wish he was a part of my life again, but I know that it may not happen. He wrote a text message to me on the day of my graduation, but more than anything, I wish that he was present at this big event in my life. He was the one who would remind me that education is important.

I do not know if I should write about my father's effect on me, it goes into me looking for approval and this modified my zest from my own God-given life force. I understand that there is a spiritual aspect to it all. I can't directly blame my parents or life circumstances. I do however have limited empathy for those who bring others down — even so, they may not have learned a better way to be optimistic. As a [future] psychiatrist, I want to help those who may want to help themselves and others but are too vulnerable. It saddens me that their willpower can be in the hands of a brain disorder and negative force.

I had an experience at a Columbia U seminar; I accompanied my friend a few years ago, and I ended up loving the school. During a seminar, I felt in my heart at that moment, and believed it was from God, that I was supposed to become a psychiatrist. I originally saw myself becoming a school psychologist or clinical psychologist. I didn't believe I was medical school material. When I was in the seminar for doctors (at the time, I was only there with my friend) I decided that I wanted to become a psychiatrist after my epiphany. I have always taken an interest in how the mind works, intakes information, and processes that information.

Antoinette Ann Acosta is a graduate of Stony Brook University. She holds a Bachelor of Arts in Psychology with a minor in English. She is currently enrolled in the Emergency Department Clinical Exposure-Mentor Program supported by Mentoring in Medicine at Mount Sinai Hospital. Her role is to shadow, teach, volunteer and more. In the past, Antoinette has interned with the Peer Health Internship program supported by the Health Education Office, Student Health Service, Counseling and Psychological Services at Stony Brook University. She was assigned to create a project that would help students understand the importance of mental health. She completed various programs during the internship, including becoming a Red Watch Band member and a Green Dot advocate. She has completed an Internship supported by the Department of English at Stony Brook University, as a student magazine writer for the campus community. Antoinette has interned with Self-Management Workshops as a peer student counselor to promote mindful decision-making and living free of worry and stress. She believes that knowledge is important and that making good life choices are important for happiness. She also relies heavily on faith.

MY NAME IS BLEAK

LACK OF VEGETATION
EXPOSED TO THE ELEMENTS
WITH
BOUTS OF DEPRESSION
MY MEAT
THERE'S REAL TENSION
BETWEEN MOOD
AND MISSION
LULLABYES
BLUE LULLABYES
HEALING TAKES
INTENTION
OH DID
I MENTION
MY
NAME
IS
BLEAK

A SILENT WAIL
Rev. Andriette Earl

As a teenager, I made two suicide attempts: first, as a high school senior, I swallowed a bottle of sleeping pills; about a year later, I swallowed another bottle of sleeping pills AND put a gun to my head and pulled the trigger.

I now see/feel these attempts at ending my life as a **silent wail**.

A "**Wail**" is a prolonged high-pitched cry of pain, grief or anger.

Attempting suicide was my deep and **SILENT WAIL**

For the Love of Life
from my heart to yours, I offer you:
"A Silent Wail"

My suicide **attempts** began within —
from deep/recurring and often hidden self-judgment,
fear and depression...
For all of my achievements, I often felt as if I'd failed.

Confirming my fear that Love was not and would never be enough,
I prepared to leave my life mission unfulfilled and **incomplete**.
I felt defeated, unworthy and disinclined to SPEAK.
I KNEW I **could not have been** the one they loved...
And in my mind, this offered certain proof
that I was rejected and **WEAK**.

I **forced** life to stand still for me
I abdicated my power to seek anything beyond.
I believed life could **NEVER-EVER** get better
I denied my heart could ever open OR even respond

Choosing to abandon my life — **MY EVERYTHING**

Has rendered me too tragic, to even speak
Or to fathom the pain and disappointment I'd cause.
Unfortunately, my choice was not at all unique

I rejected the divine calling on my life
In fact, I wished I'd **never been born**.
I doubted my life purpose and any positive destiny,
All that the future held for me, I'd already scorned.

This is bizarre — at 17???!!!
It's too soon for me/my life to have peaked
It's not that you don't truly love me
It's that I often feel unnecessary — and overly — critiqued.

The end of my life passed right before my very eyes
How could I have peaked **soooo soon**?!
What I love, I will now leave
I leave because I fear there's no space **for me** to bloom

With false courage, I open my mouth
My heart aches to tell
My "oh sooo sad" victim tale-
Yeah, even in my pain, I still got game.
(*That's pro'bly how you missed my pain…*)

I will tell it in **FULL** subjective/biased detail
Although, it's not your fault, **get ready…**
I'm sure to holler, weep and wail,
In the telling of this tale…

And yet,
All that you will ever hear, is my Silent Wail.

See, I told you I would fail.

In both the spiritual and corporate environments, Rev. Andriette Earl inspires us to our greatest yet to be. This transformational specialist is known and respected for her extraordinary discernment and her exceptional public speaking. Since 2009, Rev. Andriette has been the Founding and Senior Minister of Heart and Soul Center of Light, a Center for Spiritual Living affiliate in Oakland, California, and has honed this center into a loving, vibrant, world-class teaching and empowerment ministry. Rev. Andriette is an author, spiritual coach, mediator, and master teacher. Her knack for inspiring spiritual growth through conscious and intentional living is the foundation of her teacher portfolio. She teaches spiritual principles for effective living and offers practical tools and metaphysical processes to support self-actualization and transformation. Rev. Andriette has an unshakeable belief in the healing power of Divine Love as Law and understands how life gets to be the way it is. She consistently encourages us to reveal and express our greatest yet to BE. She is a prodigious facilitator, widely known on both coasts and abroad for her work with individuals and groups and for her dynamic and powerful messages. For six consecutive years, she was tapped to host the Essence Music Festival - Empowerment Seminars, in New Orleans with audiences of over 5,000 people. Rev. Andriette is the published author of "Embracing Wholeness: Living in Spiritual Congruence" and pens a monthly column, "From the Inside Out" for Science of Mind Magazine. Her ingenuity in creating new ways to empower was recently demonstrated in her design and development of the transformational board game, "Speak Your Word." Rev. Andriette gratefully serves as chairperson of Oakland Bay Area CARES (OBAC), a proud affiliate of the National CARES Mentoring Movement. CARES is dedicated to closing the gap between the relatively few Black mentors and millions of vulnerable children on youth-serving organizations' waiting lists yearning for a caring adult mentor.

SOMETIMES
Din E. Tolbert

Sometimes
The hurt is so heavy
I think
Will there be anything left
When the change comes
When the prayer is answered

Will there be any light in me
A smile to meet the sun
A hand for the lover to hold
Faith to look back on itself
And pity when it was younger and afraid
Will hope despise its reflection?

Sometimes
I think I am wearing
An evil man's suffering

My despair
A case of mistaken identity
And only I know it

Minister Din E. Tolbert is a sought after preacher and workshop facilitator who deals — in depth — with the social, cerebral, temporal, and spiritual parts of the individual, and teaches that Christ is Lord over them all. He was licensed for Christian ministry as an itinerant elder at The Greater Allen AME Cathedral of NY in 2003, and served for five years (2007-2012) as the Youth Pastor there. Minister Tolbert is a graduate of Cornell University (B.S., Communication '04), and Union Theological Seminary of New York City (M.Div. 2011).

IMPACT OF MENTAL ILLNESS
Angela Nilda Flores

Afraid to open her mother's bedroom door, her heart raced at the thought of her mother lying dead in bed. Taking a deep breath, she placed her fingers around the doorknob and turned it. The door would not open. This was the third day her mother remained locked in the bedroom. Kneeling down, she began looking through the bedroom door's keyhole. Screaming her mother's name, she pounded on the door with the palms of her hands and waited for her mother to respond — no response. Looking again into the keyhole, she saw empty prescription pill bottles, a knife and blood splattered over her mother's bed sheets. As her siblings began running up the staircase, she urged them to wait for her downstairs. She was afraid of letting them see their mother in this condition because she knew that doing so would lead them to suffer the same fate she had experienced many times: developing permanent and painful memories of engraved images illustrating her mother's repetitive suicide attempts.

Adrenaline rushing through her body, she struggled to get up as she desperately tried to find someone who could help. Running down the staircase, she felt the cold air brush against her face. Their family was unable to afford oil for the hot water boiler again. As a result, cold air readily passed through the walls of their poorly insulated home. Feeling the cold air penetrate through the multiple layers of sweat pants, sweatshirts and socks she was wearing, her body began to shiver uncontrollably. With an immense amount of hoarded items scattered across every room's furniture and floor, she struggled to find a phone to call 911.

Her father lay on the living room couch drunk and asleep. Hoping that he would be able to help her, she gently placed her hand on his shoulder and called his name repeatedly. After her father woke up, he struck her across the face. Falling on the floor, she hit her head against the corner of the living room table. She felt a sharp pain shoot through the back of her head. Slowly getting up, she reached with her hand to touch the back of her head only to discover blood filling her hand. As her father rolled over on the couch to fall back asleep, he yelled at her to go away and let him sleep.

Underneath a pile of unwashed clothes, she found the house phone. However, after pressing the buttons, she realized it would not power on. While searching for a charger, she noticed a stack of notices. Due to non-payment, the phone lines and electricity had been disconnected again. In desperation, she ran out of the house and into the street. Jumping in front of the first car she saw. She flagged the driver down for help. Once the ambulance arrived, her mother was hospitalized for attempted suicide. This was her sixth hospitalization that year.

As the home filled with the same healthcare providers, same police officers, and same social caseworkers, she feared having to go back to living in shelters or foster homes. Attempting to show the social worker stability within their home, she began preparing her sibling's lunches for school. Opening the refrigerator and seeing it empty, she opened the cupboards to find only expired cans of soup. Flipping her backpack upside down, she emptied it and handed her siblings the only cash she had left from waitressing that week? $8.

It was time for a change.

Wondering day after day if her mother and father would be around to live another day was not the type of lifestyle she wanted her siblings (alongside herself) to continue to live. Hugging her siblings, she reassured them that she would be there to create a healthy life for them. The instability within their broken home forced this child to assume the role of a parent. Despite having been the youngest of seven children, by age 8, this child began working to support her family financially. Immersed in poverty, this child grew up in a mentally and physically abusive home where her father suffered from alcoholism and her mother from bipolar disorder intertwined with narcissistic personality disorder. Through this child's hard work and perseverance, she became a first generation college graduate and is currently in the process of pursuing medical school.

The child in this story is me.

On February 14, 1990, I was born prematurely with sickle cell anemia, asthma and a heart murmur in San Juan, Puerto Rico. Upon immigrating to the United States, and prior to turning twelve years old, I attended 24 schools across the United States. While adapting to each school's unique curriculum, I began noticing voids within my education. Eager to learn, I immersed myself in books. With Spanish being our native language, I taught my siblings (along with myself) English as a second language. My siblings and I grew up in an unstable and abusive home heavily impacted by mental illness, poverty, crime, violence, and drugs. In order to survive, our family relied heavily on food stamps, supplemental social security income and Medicaid. Despite being the youngest of seven children, my siblings relied primarily on me for guidance, emotional, educational and financial support. I became a first generation college graduate and the first member of my family to pursue medical/graduate education. Sculpted by many adversities I've faced — some of which include the impact of domestic violence, sexual assault, and a traumatic brain injury — three years recovery time — I strive to become a physician who serves medically underserved, minority and socioeconomically disadvantaged communities through innovative research, inquisitive-driven education and compassionate patient care.

Sincerely,
Angela Nilda Flores
The Pennsylvania State University
B.S. Biology — Vertebrate Physiology

SCATTERED WHOLENESS
Rev. Stephanie Angelique

Sometimes…it's not about how you appear to those watching.
It's hard being a winner, when losing is the only thing you see.

I work hard to make the mirror my friend.

Running from DNA
That never fails to meet me at the finish line

Denying I was like him
Yet…I write Haiku…Prose…Verses
While…Methodically Deciphering Sacred Text, unintentionally
Because…Parables and Proverbs is the language
he taught me to live by
But…Living is the hardest thing to do, once I realize
So…I stop praying, to not wake up
Because…I don't want despair to turn into a plan

I work hard to make the mirror my friend.

Clinician, Heal Thyself
Preacher, Restore Thyself
Woman, Hug Thyself
Daughter, Father Thyself
Believer, Encourage Thyself
Wait…
This is not how this works…
This is not how any of this works…
Most of the time
Sigh…
So, I surrender…(breathe)…!!!!!!!!

Forgiveness apprehends my thinking
So, that the healing can begin

God is forgiven for not being the God
my Sunday school teacher said He was.
The True God Stands Up...and She Stands Strong.

Daddy is forgiven for conceiving me in his image.
The Full Image is Complicatedly Beautiful...
and that my soul knows well.
Self is forgiven for wanting to fit into a self that I will never be.
The True Self Is Worth the battle to Be...
And Being Me is what I am blessed to Be.

I work hard to make the mirror my friend.

—Rev. Stephanie Angelique Duzant

Rev. Stephanie A. Duzant is of Caribbean American heritage with roots from the U.S. Virgin Islands and St. Martin/Saint Maarten of the Dutch and French Antilles. She is an ordained itinerant elder with the New York Annual Conference African Methodist Episcopal Church. She serves as an associate minister, and the chairperson of the Social Action Ministry at St. Matthew's Community A.M.E. Church, where the Rev. Dr. Andrea M. Hargett is the pastor. Rev. Duzant earned a Master's of Divinity degree from Union Theological Seminary in New York City. Her area of focus was Biblical and Womanist studies. Rev. Duzant is also a retired Social Worker who holds a Master's of Social Work degree from Fordham University, with a clinical focus and specialization in Children and Families. Rev. Duzant strives to answer God's call to help strengthen families and bring communities together.

voices

was born under a bad star
they just don't understand
waking up never knowing
if you can
hold on to this thin thread
is my daily hope
hiding in my special darkness
day into night to cope
try so hard to draw folks near
as they move further away
soon everyone will know
there will be dues to pay
for all the hurts this soul
now mindlessly bare
from the countless nights waking
from the same nightmare
no more suffering in silence
no more hiding my woe
gotta lash out to make
my pain show
that fate forced me to
aimlessly roam
searching for the place
once
called
home

WIN!
Donicia Carlos

How many times are you going to screw your life up and the lives of others? How many times are you going to apologize for your behavior? How many times are you going to deny who you are? How long are you going to hold onto that guilt and not forgive yourself? Don't you know your flaws don't define you? How much longer are you going to lie to yourself and others by saying everything is ok when it's not?

How many more jobs can you lose? How much more compulsive can you become? Can your credit score plummet into the abyss any further? Will your lights be off or will you be evicted because you spent the rent on everything but the rent? Don't you know there is no shame in being depressed and bipolar and OCD and schizophrenic? Are you ever going to come to grips with it? Are you ever going to stop hiding behind the layers and layers of masks you've created thinking they were going to save you? Don't you realize those masks are what took you to the edge of the cliff and made you jump into that bottle chasing those 75 pills?

How long are you going to hide in the house away from the world? How long are you going to sabotage every relationship you get your hand on? How long will the circus be in town? You know the one where there's always a fire to put out that you've created. Oh, wait, that's not really a fire, it's just you moving your feet around to kick up dust. How long will drama seep into the core of your fiber soon replacing your rational thought process?

How long will your children hope this is the last time you will do something to them only an enemy would do to them and not their mother? How long will your mother PRAY for you hoping GOD will work a miracle in your life and just change who are so she can stop bailing you out and feeling her own guilt for something she has no control over?

How long will you be in denial about your life? How long will you lie about what getting to the root of your fear is about? How long will your fear run and rule your life? How long will you distance yourself from yourself, your real authentic self? How long will you let your talents go untapped? How long will you play it safe and be mediocre? How long will you be unstoppable? How long will you be a victim?

How long will you deny your greatness? How long will you let bipolar disorder and depression define you? How long will you let the shame and stigma control you? How long will you let your potential be held hostage by a condition in your life not the condition of your life?

I'm Donicia and I live with mental illness. I am not my condition. It is a part of my life but it is not my life. I have chosen to live and define me for me.

—*Donicia Carlos*

Donicia Carlos, Founder, LEAP — Lifting Education Activating Parents founded to inspire authentic partnerships between schools, families and the community that result in parent and community involvement, school support and increased student achievement and performance

THE LIGHT
Kenneth Nelson

Once it offered warmth, comfort, peace, and tranquility.
Only one day it began to feel like the onset of senility.
Now, it's just an old wilted and tattered blanket.
That began to feel just like the lining of a casket.
Often engulfing me from the bottom of my feet
to the top of my head.
Making it seem like it was totally impossible
just to get out of bed.
A home that was once full of laughter, and joy
and was airy and bright.
Suddenly turned into a little gray room
devoid of all hope and any kind of light.
Leaving only the dismal shadow of oneself.
Attempting to stash these feelings
away on the back of the shelf.
I am talking, I am screaming but there is no one listening.
Surrounded only by the sounds of the radiator hissing.
This house full of gloom and appears so bleak
Seems to contain it all.
Trapping me inside of its gripping dark walls.
The air around me was thick and musty
making it terribly hard for me to breath.
Hearing the sounds of outside, but being unable to go,
seemed hard to conceive.
There was this and only this, day after day
infested with crippling fear.
Days turned into weeks, weeks into months
then it became an entire year
The wolf dressed in sheep's clothing continuing to reappear
But one day there was a knock on the door, I heard it, loud and clear
Although it was as soft as a whispering bell
My body said answer it but my mind said what the hell
It felt like a weight keeping me in place,

Like a dull forgotten monument
A self-induced torture and a soul full of torment
Now it was early Spring
on a bright and sunny Tuesday afternoon
The birds were boasting their freedom
singing to their own tunes
The knocking returned, only louder that day
Now on this day my feet hit the floor
My hands reached out for the door
And as the door opened I heard a voice say
My child I have sent you the light
To guide you on your way!

Kenneth Todd (KT) Nelson, is a new millennium social activist and actor. He is a native of Winston-Salem, North Carolina. At the age of 15, he became focused on responding to such societal ills as racism and violence. As his passion grew for wanting to help and lend support to other teenagers who suffered from a myriad of challenges in their lives, young Kenneth started a nonprofit organization called CARV (Children Against Racism and Violence). After the loss of both of his parents within a short two-year time span, Nelson was determined to fight and press his way toward wholeness and healing. Rather than let his depression define him, he decided to take action and once again help others who were also suffering and being consumed by feelings of depression and despair. Nelson merged his experiences as a community activist and actor to create a telling documentary called "Faces of Darkness." In this cinematic project, KT serves as the co-creator, executive producer, and director of this compelling film which shines a spotlight on the crippling effects of depression and anxiety amongst African American men. KT eventually co-founded the Knights Thriving (KT) Foundation that stresses the importance of education, leadership, health, community, brotherhood and fine arts for young boys. Through the Knights Thriving Foundation, Nelson and his partners work with local communities and schools to guide children in directions that will lead them to meaningful experiences and successful lives.

city poet

body stands motionless
facing the rising sun
day for this poet
just begun
torrent of words now
fill the air
intelligent questions
met with a stare
pain in the words
this poet use
cause some to wonder
others to muse
why destiny picked this
person to rhyme
plea to deaf ears
voice lost in time
the poet as a child
not long ago
ardently chased the
leaves that blow
the only joy in
life today
being free
to do
and
say

I was the first African-American male valedictorian in the history of my high school. I was voted Homecoming King/Mr. Uniondale! To top off my high school experience, I was accepted to Harvard University and started college at 17. I made everyone from the pastor of my church to the teachers in my school to my close friends proud. I got great grades in my first few quizzes and quickly made friends. I joined the Harvard cheerleading squad — 200 pounds solid, I was able to toss cheerleaders in one hand. I was also nominated Outstanding Male Sophomore by my peers. However, my life was about to take a 180° turn.

A few weeks into school, one September evening in 1998, my room began to close in on me, my palms became sweaty and my stomach turned nauseous. I rushed back to my dorm; I was having a panic attack. A year and a half later, I had a full-blown manic episode — both seeing Jesus on a Cambridge street corner and hearing cars talk on the same night. I was hospitalized for two weeks and began taking psychiatric medication.

I went back to school 18 months later. I gained 60 pounds because of the medication, my knees swelled, I became sluggish. I could not stay focused on my textbooks for more than five minutes at a time. I quit the cheerleading squad. I left school and moved back home. I worked at a bank while seeing a psychiatrist and therapist twice a week. I spent a lot of time alone.

I finally went back to Harvard to finish my degree and immediately went on to Columbia University for two master's degrees. In 2007, I began working in higher education as a college advisor. For five years, I was asking students what they wanted to do with their lives, but I was not doing what I wanted to do with mine.

In 2012, I put in my 30-day notice and immediately joined the National Alliance on Mental Illness' In Our Own Voice Program. In 2013, I began presenting in schools as the NAMI Queens/Nassau Let's Talk Mental Illness™ (LTMI) presenter, and in 2017, I launched my school-based program, *Breaking Through Stigma: The Highs and Lows of Mental Health*. Through my work with students, I have now spoken in over 150 educational institutions to over 50,000 students.

The first half of my life has been defined by mental illness. In speaking with thousands of people living with mental illness and the family members of people living with mental illness, I know many others do the same thing I was doing — we confuse ourselves with our condition and become defined by it. As a result, we define what we can and cannot do by our condition. We make all of our accomplishments and failures the result of mental illness. We see our whole lives through a singular lens. But, it does not have to be this way.

When I speak at schools, colleges, organizations, and companies, I share the message that it's okay to talk, it's okay to seek help and there is hope. We are not our labels, nor our flaws, or faults. In fact, it is our challenges that are clues to our greatest success. I still take medication. I still experience the dips of depression and anxiety so intense that I have to leave crowded rooms. But, what I have realized is: I am not my meds nor my doctor appointments. I am not bipolar — I am acceptance, I am Hakeem Rahim.

Nadir

Hakeem Rahim

Depression so real
I was down and doubled over
My couch my coffin,
Soon to be buried with my dreams

Lethargy stitched into brown suede cushions:
Now a shade of my brightest self

I lay in silence,
Sleep did not call my name

Tears lingering in the corners of my eyes
Slowly drop towards the ground

The sounds of hopelessness
Creeps into every crevice of my mind

There is so much to live for
The lowest point of my life speaks death

Yet even in these low moments
Faith whispers resurrection was possible
Hope my kite can withstand chaotic winds
Strength to climb from the pit of my fears

The key to recovery accepting I was depressed
Come what may I had to rise to my feet

Come what may I had to give up depression's seat
Come what may I had to get up and walk

I Was Dying On The Inside
Expanded Susan L. Taylor Article
Reprinted With Permission

Susan L. Taylor, the beautiful, flawless face of *Essence Magazine* for 27 years was synonymous with beauty, intelligence, grace and even as some may describe now, "black girl magic" before the term was ever thought of. Susan was the editorial director of *Essence* for eight years, and before that was editor-in-chief for 19 years. In her monthly column, "In the Spirit," she used the platform to speak to millions of black women on a personal level. And her message to all was simple: "Love yourself." Those of us who read her monthly column know that the now 71-year-old Taylor's journey to self-love and success was filled with her own personal struggle, with insecurities, anxiety, doubt and fear.

"Menopause was a major emotional challenge for me. I felt like things were falling apart. My memory and fluidity in speaking were challenged. It was as though I was in a downward spiral, sinking further and further into a sadness that I couldn't pull myself out of," says the CEO of the National CARES Mentoring Movement, which she founded as Essence CARES. "My thoughts were foggy; my speech unclear. Constantly focused on what I believed I was losing only magnified my fears and sadness.

> Depression affects between 17-20 million Americans a year. Data from a study published by the Center for Disease Control (CDC) found that women (4 percent vs. 2.7 percent of men) and African-Americans (4 percent) are significantly more likely to report major depression than whites (3.1 percent). But the CDC also finds that just 7.6 percent of African-Americans sought treatment for depression compared to 13.6 percent of the general population in 2011. Fear, embarrassment and the stigma in the Black community against counseling (outside of the church that is) keep many of us who actually need professional services from seeking them.

Writer and former colleague of Taylor, Linda Villanova sums it up best: Success can come with a price. We're the first to arrive and the last to leave as we grind through 10-hour workdays. We're the ones everybody relies on — first at work, then after hours during the second shift of home and family time. We work ourselves almost literally "to death" especially now during this economic storm. Or for some of us, we "feel" like we have to continue to be the "superwoman."

Taylor says, "My sadness, feeling depressed was the result of giving myself to multiple, competing responsibilities and pressures, before giving myself to me! Everything for *Essence*, for family, friends, the community — but taking time for needed rest, renewal, down time had fallen off my schedule. This is an unfortunate tradition among Black women. We take great pride in giving — even to the point of exhaustion. We come out of the womb believing we are here to serve others, when serving is all of our responsibility, for both women and men, after serving ourselves, which is not selfish, but smart. My mother's constant refrain was, 'Charity begins at home'."

Taylor recounts that for a time during menopause she forgot what she knew: that we have specific needs at each stage of our lives, and exercise, meditation, quiet time to restore must be the constants for us to maintain balance, give from our overflow, not from a place of weariness and emptiness. "At home, there were times I would be in tears, feeling overwhelmed, on edge, not wanting to be married anymore — though my beloved Khephra is the best man I know," she said.

"In public, I wore the mask — at work, traveling, speaking before thousands of people, I had a smile pasted on my face, but felt like I was dying on the inside. We Black women know how to look good while feeling bad. Menopause taught me to have respect for all of me — the gift of my body, my feelings, for hormonal shifts that are a natural part of life. In retrospect, it was a time of tremendous growth for me. Going through menopause, I couldn't ignore myself. I saw clearly that to bring my life into balance, I would have to learn to move at a pace of grace, become fluent about my feelings, allowing them and trusting to be with them and give voice to them without shame."

"Spending quiet time, time looking within, asking myself the critical questions in the quiet: *How are you doing — really?*" "*What are you feeling?*" "*What must you do to root peace, joy and wholeness in your psyche and soul during part of your journey?"* Pondering these questions during quiet time, which I had unwittingly surrendered to busyness, brought me to the understanding that pain is information, often how the Holy Spirit speaks to us, awakens us to ourselves, how we find our way home to ourselves and to God." Taylor says, "It was a blessing to be able to write about my emotional pain and the lessons I was learning. Sharing them with *Essence* readers helped me heal and encourage others to be present, comfortable with change and courageous in honoring ourselves throughout the many stages of our amazing lives."

—Susan L. Taylor Founder & CEO, *National CARES Mentoring Movement* and Editor-in-Chief Emerita of *Essence Magazine.*

Susan L. Taylor, best-selling author of four books, and editor of eight others, is a fourth-generation entrepreneur, who grew up in Harlem working in her father's clothing store. At 24, she founded her own cosmetics company, which led to the beauty editor's position at Essence, the publication she would go on to shape into a world-renown brand with more than 8 million readers. It was that enterprising spirit wedded to a deep love for her community that led to the founding of the National CARES Mentoring Movement in 2005 as Essence CARES. With local affiliates in 58 cities, National CARES has recruited, trained and deployed more than 140,000 mentors to schools and youth-support and mentoring organizations like Big Brothers, Big Sisters, as well as in its own culturally rooted, academic and social transformational initiatives. A community-mobilization movement, National CARES is the only organization dedicated to providing mentoring, healing and wellness services on a national scale for Black children. A lifelong activist who has worked to ensure people across the globe, from South Africa to those who struggled in the wake of Katrina, Susan says, securing our children is her highest calling and the big business of Black America today.

DEPRESSION CALLS

MELANCHOLY
CAVE DWELLING
MIND SWELLING
CAN'T HOLD A THOUGHT
OR REMEMBER WHAT
THE GOOD BOOK TAUGHT
MIND RACING
HARD TIME
FACING
WHAT HERITAGE TRACING
SAID
YOU'VE COME THROUGH
BUT YET CAN'T IGNORE
DEPRESSION'S CALL

STARTS REAL SMALL
SUBTLE PUSH
TO PULL ME DOWN
SOMETHING CRAWLING
ON MY SKIN
OR FROM WITHIN
THIS
CAULDRON VORTEX
QUICKSAND
SPIRIT SLAMMED
BY MOOD
TAKING CUES
FROM
WHEREVER
WHENEVER

IS THIS FACT
OR FICTION
THAT I CAN DO
ALL THINGS
WHEN THE PENDULUM
SWINGS
HUMANITY
THE FIXED POINT
I MUST
DECIDE
NOT GOING
TO HIDE
CREATED TO BARE FRUIT
STOP LOOKING
START SEEING
I'M NOT
THE ONLY ONE
DEPRESSION CALLS
JUST THAT
THERE'S
DIFFERENT
HUES
OF
THE
BLUES

Contributors

Antoinette Ann Acosta
Dr. Sonia R. Banks
Donicia Carlos
Rev. Stephanie Angelique Duzant
Rev. Andriette Earl
Sabrina Evans Ellis
Khafre Evelyn
Angela Nilda Flores
AGL
Kenneth Nelson
Hakeem Rahim
Susan L. Taylor
Rev. Din Tolbert
Eulani Tucker
Rev. Dr. Alfonso Wyatt
Ouida C. Wyatt

Other books by Alfonso & Ouida Wyatt

Soul Be Free Poems Prose Prayers
Soul Be Free II
Mentoring From The Inside Out: Healing Boys Transforming Men
Before You Jump The Broom: Clean Up Your Room
Leadership By Numbers: For God's People Who Count
Madd Truth: Lasting Lessons For Students of Life

Ouida and Alfonso Wyatt, partners in marriage and friendship for 43 years, are called to use their gifts, talents, and lived experience to explore ways to creatively address the most pressing needs of the human condition. Ouida is the visionary behind the Soul Be Free series. Alfonso Wyatt is a respected mentor and public theologian.

43

Mental Health Resource

NAMI, the National Alliance on Mental Illness, is the nation's largest grassroots mental health organization dedicated to building better lives for the millions of Americans affected by mental illness. What started as a small group of families gathered around a kitchen table in 1979 has blossomed into the nation's leading voice on mental health. Today, we are an association of hundreds of local affiliates, state organizations and volunteers who work in your community to raise awareness and provide support and education that was not previously available to those in need. NAMI relies on gifts and contributions to support our important work:

We educate. Offered in thousands of communities across the United States through NAMI State Organizations and NAMI Affiliates, our education programs ensure hundreds of thousands of families, individuals and educators get the support and information they need.

We advocate. NAMI shapes national public policy for people with mental illness and their families and provides volunteer leaders with the tools, resources and skills necessary to save mental health in all states.

We listen. Our toll-free NAMI HelpLine allows us to respond personally to hundreds of thousands of requests each year, providing free referral, information and support—a much-needed lifeline for many.

We lead. Public awareness events and activities, including Mental Illness Awareness Week and NAMIWalks, successfully fight stigma and encourage understanding. NAMI works with reporters on a daily basis to make sure our country understands how important mental health is.
—taken from NAMI Website under title Mental Health Resource

800-950-NAMI
info@nami.org
M-F, 10 AM - 6 PM ET
Find help in crisis text "NAMI" to 741741

www.ingramcontent.com/pod-product-compliance
Lightning Source LLC
Chambersburg PA
CBHW022343280326
41934CB00006B/753